BUTTERFLIES
& MANDALAS

An Adult Coloring Book
with Positive Affirmations

Transcendental
Coloring

I AM BEAUTIFUL

I AM JOYFUL

I AM STRONG

I AM CARING

I MATTER

I AM SUCCESSFUL

I AM BRIGHT

I AM THOUGHTFUL

I DESERVE WONDERFUL THINGS

I AM GRATEFUL

I AM HOPEFUL

I AM A GOOD FRIEND

I AM OPTIMISTIC

I AM IN CHARGE

I NEVER GIVE UP

I AM ACCEPTING

I AM CALM

I AM A GIFT

I AM COURAGEOUS

I AM POSITIVE

I AM COURAGEOUS

I EMBRACE MY HEART

I AM CREATIVE

I AM ENTHUSIASTIC

I FORGIVE MYSELF

I AM HEALTHY

I AM AWESOME

I AM PERSISTENT

I AM PATIENT

I INSPIRE OTHERS

I TAKE PLEASURE

I AM LOYAL

I AM PEACEFUL

I AM FOCUSED

I AM LOVED

THANK YOU!

WE HOPE YOU ENJOYED coloring all the beautiful butterflies and mandalas while contemplating the affirmations. It has been shown that positive thinking and repeating affirmative words work to make our lives better. How much more effective must affirmations be when accompanied by the creative flow of doing colorful artwork as you meditate upon them? Hopefully, this book has helped you achieve the self-expression and peace of mind you seek.

If you have a moment, please help others enjoy this book! Post a review online and tell them why you loved this book!

MORE CREATIVE COLORING BOOKS FROM TRANSCENDENTAL COLORING GROUP:
Please visit: http://bit.ly/TransColor

Butterflies & Mandalas
Dragonflies & Mandalas
Pretty Shoes
Hummingbirds & Hamsas
My Big Bad Breakup
Awesome Zentangle Animals
Coloring for Book Lovers

PUBLISHED BY CAJUN HOT PRESS
BUTTERFLIES & MANDALAS
ISBN-13: 978-1517261429
ISBN-10: 1517261422
All rights reserved
Copyright © October 2015 by Cajun Hot Press, LLC

Cover art designed by Nina Bruhns.

Cajun Hot Press
October 2015